123443

Fraiberg

Every child's

Every Child's Birthright

Every Child's Birthright

In Defense of Mothering

Selma Fraiberg

Basic Books, Inc., Publishers   New York

Library of Congress Cataloging in Publication Data

Fraiberg, Selma H.
  Every child's birthright.

  Includes bibliographical references.
    1. Parent and child.   2.   Child development.
I.   Title.
HQ755.85.F7   301.42′7   77-74574
ISBN: 0-465-02132-8

For Jennie, Dora, and Lisa

CONTENTS

Preface and Acknowledgments

IN PSYCHOLOGY, as in any branch of knowledge, a time lag may exist between what is known, what is stored in the library, and the uses of that knowledge in the conduct of human affairs. During the past three decades the study of human infancy by developmental psychologists has given us stunning insights into the origins of love and the formation of human bonds. The evidence from diverse studies and schools of psychology converges and has led to this consensus: the human capacity to love and to make enduring partnerships in love is formed in infancy, the embryonic period of development. The child learns to love through his first human partners, his parents. We can look upon this miraculous occurrence as a "gift" of love to the baby. We should also regard it as a right, a birthright for every child.

"Mothering," that old fashioned word, is the nurturing of the human potential of every baby to love, to trust, and to bind himself to human partnerships in a lifetime of love. Under extraordinary circumstances, when a baby has been deprived of a mother or a mother substitute through adversity or disaster or the indifference of his society, we have found that the later capacity of that child to commit himself to love, to partners in love, and to the human community will be diminished or depleted. Unfortunately, the number of such children is growing in our society. In less extraordinary circumstances we are seeing a devaluation of parental nurturing and commitment to babies in our society which may affect the quality and stability of the child's human attachments in ways that cannot yet be predicted.

It is my hope in writing this book to create a bridge—admittedly a narrow bridge—between "what is known" and stored in the library and "what is practiced" in the rearing of infants and in the social institutions which minister to the welfare of infants and young children. This small book cannot do justice to the scientific issues and their implications for children. It can only serve to raise questions and to examine beliefs, attitudes, practices, and policies which affect the development of infants and young children in our society.

The format of this book follows the story as it emerged for me as a researcher and clinician in infant development. Chapters I and II describe those parts of it that came from infant research in human and animal psychology. Chapters III, IV, and V examine the implications of these findings for infants and the social institutions which serve families and their children. The story is a sobering one. The reader may be relieved to know in advance that Chapter VI ends in a spirit of optimism. That's what happens when babies are the subject of a book.

I am indebted to many colleagues who have helped me in the preparation of this manuscript. For research assistance, I am grateful to John Bennett and Susan Darrow. Joseph and Edna Adelson, Clarice Freud, Harold and Vivian Shapiro read and criticized early drafts and brought their own expert knowledge to me in areas where I cannot claim authority. My thanks to Martha Springer for generous consultation. For fastidious preparation of this manuscript I thank Anita Vander Haagen, Adele Wilson, and Laura Hersey.

My gratitude as always goes to my husband, Louis, who read and criticized several versions of this manuscript. Midge Decter of Basic Books brought wise counsel and her own exceptional editorial gifts to the preparation of the final manuscript.

Preface and Acknowledgments

An earlier version of Chapter II appeared in *Commentary* in 1967 under the title, "The Origins of Human Bonds." Substantial parts of Chapter III appeared in *Redbook Magazine* in February 1975 with the title, "The Right to Know Love." I am grateful to *Commentary* and to *Redbook* for permission to include this material in this volume.

Every Child's Birthright

CHAPTER I

Birthrights

THE BIRTHRIGHTS which are the subject of this chapter are the rights of infants. They are also the rights of parents. The birth of a child is a celebration of love. Under all favorable circumstances this celebration leads to the conferring of love upon the baby, which is to say that the child is granted full citizenship in the human community. There are ancient traditions which have bound the baby and his parents together from the first hours of life, traditions deeply rooted in our biological heritage. It was not known until our time why the traditions existed or whether in fact the human family should be bound to them. But the evidence that now emerges from a large body of scientific work is incontrovertible: the traditions themselves were "intended" to insure the love bonds between the baby and his parents.

If we now understand the origins and evolution of human bonds, we are indebted for this knowledge to children who were robbed of human partners in their early childhood. The children of war, tyranny, and human disasters who survived without parents or parent substitutes gave their own terrible testimony: the absence of human partners in infancy and early childhood produced a child who had diminished capacity or no capacity for forming human attachments in later childhood or adult life. The best gifts of the psychotherapist could not give these children, who were robbed of their birthrights, that which every baby normally receives in the human family in the first years of life. No one could fill the vacancy within.

Later, in Chapter II, I shall speak of these children. For the problem we are examining in this chapter, it may be enough to say here that it was the "lost children" who had been robbed of their capability for love who caused the scientific community in child development to ask an elementary question: "What goes on between an ordinary baby and his parents that produces a member of the human family who is capable of love that endures?"

Many of the answers have emerged gradually in the past forty years. They are the result of studies which took place during the past two decades. We have identified a language of love, a "dialogue" between the baby and his parents which begins in the first hours of life and becomes elaborated in ordinary experience during the first two years of life. We have decoded the eye language, the smile language, the need language and a large number of signs and signals which had previously gone unremarked and unexamined, because of their "ordinariness." [1]

We have learned how the love bonds are formed, and we have a map for ourselves which shows the development of these bonds in the course of infancy.

And finally, a sobering discovery: we have learned that the human qualities of enduring love and commitment to love are forged during the first two years of life. On this point there is a consensus among scientists from a wide range of disciplines.

We are living in times when there are voices which denigrate the human family and even cry for its dissolution or its recomposition. I cannot identify the voices of infant psychologists among them.

This book is intended for all those radicals, like myself, who think that our survival as a human community may depend as much upon our nurture of love in infancy and childhood as upon the protection of our society from external threats.

In the pages that follow I shall attempt to sketch the story of the development of human attachments in infancy. The story, as it takes form in my mind, wants to follow its own path, one that converges with folk wisdom at many points, touches upon our biological heritage, and brings in some of the central findings in developmental research.

Folk Wisdom and the Rearing of Babies

My grandmother, if she were alive, would be astonished to read the reports of infant psychologists in our time.

"Love begins in a mother's arms! Did someone just *discover* this?"

She would be amused by the jargon we have invented to describe the process of mother-infant attachment. "Tactile and kinesthetic stimulation." "Mutual gaze patterns." "Visual stimulus of the mother's face." "Auditory feedback." "Differential stimuli for smiling."

She would be pleased and not surprised to find her own maternal wisdom vindicated by contemporary science.

The baby can see soon after he's born? I always knew that.

The baby smiles to his mother's voice at four weeks? I told the doctors that myself but they wouldn't believe me.

The baby recognizes his mother and prefers her before six months of age? Why not? After all, she's his mother!

Stranger reactions at twelve months? Did the doctors just find out?

A baby should be comforted when he cries? What mother doesn't know that?

While my grandmother and I would see eye to eye on a number of major issues in infant psychology we would run into problems on rules of evidence. "If I *know*," her argument would go, "Why do I have to prove it?"

We can argue, of course, that my grandmother's folk wisdom has a scientific rationale of its own kind, too. It represents the "findings" of "an experiment" of colossal numbers, the natural experiment of the human race over countless generations. The "experiment" moved with glacial slowness over time; at stake was the survival of the species. The nurturing of an infant was imbedded in traditions which were held sacred in each society. The traditions themselves were derived from biological imperatives. While there were variants in the practices of infant rearing between one branch of the human family and another, one can argue from contemporary studies that all of the branches had more in common in their practices than these differences would suggest.

Watching films of a Philippine tribe, the Tasaday, on TV, I was impressed to see glimpses of infant and child rearing in this "stone-age" tribe which varied only in minor details from "traditional" practices in tribes thousands of miles away, geographically separated by oceans and mountains and economically separated by agricultural and technological attainments which placed them tens of thousands of years apart.

And between the Tasaday practices of infant rearing and those of my grandmother there were not significant differences if we put aside the advances in medical science that my grandmother had available to her.

In my grandmother's time, a baby was delivered at home with a midwife attending and a doctor on call for emergencies. The woman in labor was metaphorically embraced in the arms of her family. Her husband could be there, her mother, women of the family, perhaps—all participants in an ancient rite which united the tribe in a miraculous experience.

The risks to the baby and to the mother were very large even in this era of medicine. I will not argue for home deliveries. But in the ancient tradition the birth of a baby was an exalted experience within the human family. The baby himself was delivered and placed immediately into the waiting arms of his mother. With this embrace, he was initiated into the human community.

Nearly all babies were breast-fed in my grandmother's time and in her community. They were probably breast-fed for a year or longer. And since the breast and the embrace were one for the baby, he experienced the satisfaction of hunger and the enjoyment of all senses, which we call bliss, in his mother's arms.

Decisions regarding the nutritional needs of the growing baby were largely eliminated for the mother since the self-regulating system of breast-feeding under normal circumstances provided adequacy. Similarly, the inexperienced mother did not need to provide extraordinary sterile conditions for the conduct of the feeding.

During the period of breast feeding, the mother and the baby were largely bound to each other. Older children in the family could (and did) take over baby care during many hours of the day, but the institution of the hired babysitter was largely unknown. The breast feeding mother, then as now, could not be separated from her baby for long intervals. This means, of course, that the baby rarely was cared for by a stranger, and was mainly nurtured by his mother.

Neither my grandmother nor any other woman in her generation had a scientific rationale for her infant rearing practices. She could not have told you that all of her traditional practices were "designed" to promote intimacy between an

7

infant and his mother, and that this intimacy led to the unfolding of a biological program which under all favorable conditions established stable and enduring love bonds.

My grandmother would not have been pleased to learn that her infant rearing practices were very close, in principle, to those of a remote village in Mexico, Africa, or India. She was herself literate, respectful of medical science, and vigilant against the microbes that threatened the health of babies. She was also a militant suffragette, but her radical feminism did not alter her methods of infant rearing one iota.

She was, then, a modern up-to-date woman of the first decade of this century, and she would be offended by the comparisons which I find between her practices in infant rearing and those of a "primitive" tribe, as we used to say. She would have found the mothers of such tribes uneducated, superstitious, wanting in hygiene and good housekeeping standards. Any resemblance between their nurture of infants and her own would not have interested her. How else, she would have asked, can you rear a baby given the fact that all babies are constitutionally alike the world over?

Since I do not share my grandmother's prejudices against "primitive tribes" I have allowed my imagination to create an impossible situation in which three contemporary tribes from undeveloped regions are brought together with a modern industrialized tribe for a fruitful exchange on the subject of infant rearing. For this purpose I have invented an International Congress of Mothers and Babies and have recorded the proceedings to advance our discussion.

Proceedings of the First International Congress of Mothers and Babies

Delegations from four geographically isolated regions are invited to this Congress. Tribe A has its home in a rural region in Mexico. Tribe B has its origins in Africa. Tribe C occupies a remote village in India. Tribe D lives in a village in North America.

Mothers with infants under three are encouraged to bring them along to the sessions of the Congress.

INTRODUCTIONS

At the usual informal get-together that precedes all such Congresses, it is impressive to see that each tribe has its own style of carrying babies. Tribe A carries its babies in a shawl, ingeniously wrapped around the baby so that he is suspended at breast level. Tribe B mothers suspend the small baby from a shoulder sling. Tribe C carries its babies snugly wrapped at the breast in a fold of the mother's garment. Tribe D carries its babies (a) in the arms of the mother, (b) in a basket with handles, (c) in a back-pack, (d) in a wheeled carriage, (e) in a molded plastic seat.

It is immediately apparent that in mode of infant transport Tribes A, B and C, though geographically isolated, have more in common with each other than with Tribe D. The reasons are also apparent. Since nearly all of the babies in Tribes A, B, and C are breast-fed, the modes of carrying the baby were "invented" to bring the baby close to the source of supply.

During the usual inaugural speeches of a conference, the four tribes outdo each other in praising infancy and motherhood. But no one can match the record of Tribe D. In Tribe D the exaltation of child and mother is celebrated in sacred rites. No candidate for public office in this tribe can be elected unless he kisses at least one baby in front of a camera. Motherhood is celebrated once a year on a special day called "Mother's Day." On this day pilgrims line the highways in bumper-to-bumper traffic jams to bring floral offerings and other gifts to mothers.

SESSION #1: INFANT HEALTH

Spokesmen from each tribe present their latest statistics on infant mortality and infant disease. Charts, graphs, and tables are projected on a screen and the nimble-witted who can read these things can easily see that everyone is lying a little bit. With a statistical correction for tribal vanity, it can be seen that Tribes A, B, and C lag far behind Tribe D in eradicating death and illness in infants, but their death and disease rates are not significantly different from those of impoverished families within Tribe D.[2]

The Conference is off to a bad start. It is not a good idea to bring in statistical charts at the start of a meeting. Some delegates from all four tribes are dozing. Others are kept in an alert state through the tending to complaining babies and the pursuit of restless toddlers.

A glance at the program will tell us that the next topics on the agenda should be of more general interest to the audience.

SESSION #2: TACTILE AND KINESTHETIC STIMULATION IN INFANCY

"Tactile and Kinesthetic Stimulation in Infancy" is a lecture given by a distinguished Tribe D psychiatrist.

Much of the doctor's speech cannot be easily rendered in the polylingual simultaneous translation. When it is finally summarized, the mothers of tribes A, B, and C are dumbfounded to hear that while they have been holding their babies, nursing their babies, and transporting their babies they have been giving tactile and kinesthetic stimulation to the baby which is essential for his neurophysiological maturation *and* for his emotional well-being.[3]

"I never realized that!" says a Tribe B mother to her neighbor. "It just goes to show. Even at a lousy conference like this you can always come away with a new idea."

SESSION #3: FEEDING YOUR BABY

Feeding your baby brings about lively debate among the delegates. Nearly all the mothers in Tribes A, B, and C breast feed their babies. But there is disagreement among them on the optimal time for weaning them from the breast. Tribe B weans its babies around two years of age. Tribe A regards this as "early weaning," a barbarous practice, and ascribes the vigor and longevity of its tribe to weaning between the ages of three and five. Tribe B argues that when it comes to vigor and longevity, it can match any other tribe at the Congress.

The Tribe D delegation applauds breast feeding "whenever possible." Mainly Tribe D babies are fed a scientific formula in plastic bottles. The vigor and longevity of Tribe D is cited in support of the scientific formula in plastic bottles. A minority of women in the Tribe D delegation argue the merits of the plastic bottle for those women who do not want to be "tied down." It is not good for some Tribe D mothers to be "tied down." It is not good for a Tribe D baby to have a mother who is tied down. A mother who is tied down might become neurotic, and her nerves would affect the baby.

In the polylingual translation, the idiom "tied down" is rendered literally, and the delegations from Tribes A, B, and C listen with grave and sorrowful faces. Evidently in Tribe D a mother who wished to breast feed her baby was bound hand and foot, and it was to escape this brutal and barbaric treatment that some women in Tribe D resorted to plastic bottles.

SESSION #4: EDUCATION FOR PARENTHOOD

Education for parenthood is illuminating, and the arguments are sharp. In Tribes A, B, and C little girls and boys become "child nurses" at an early age. This is shown in a movie. Little girls are seen at play with an infant wrapped in a shawl or a sling, snuggled against the chest. Little boys carry baby brothers and sisters in an improvised sling on the chest or on the shoulders, depending upon the age of the infant. All this takes place under the watchful eyes of the mother. At the age of five, most children in these tribes know "the right way to carry babies," "how to soothe the baby," "how to change a diaper," "how to wash the baby." Pictures are flashed on a screen which show a small girl toting a baby nearly as large as herself, a small boy playing tag with his friends, hoisting an infant occasionally to free his arms.

There are shocked murmurs from the Tribe D delegation. Among themselves, the women of Tribe D whisper "exploitation of children," "no time to be a child," "no time to play." The delegation from Tribes A, B, and C, aware of dissenting noises from Tribe D but not knowing why, sum up their education for parenthood with acerbity. Their methods, they argue, are the same methods which their ancestors have employed for centuries. The mothers of Tribes A, B, and C had carried their younger brothers and sisters because it was a privilege. As for the end result of this education one could see for oneself that every boy and girl will have learned how to take care of a baby when the time comes to bring one's own children into the world.

Tribe D now has the floor. This presentation is illustrated with videotape. In Tribe D little girls and boys are prepared for parenthood through play. This is so they will learn that parenthood is fun. Between the ages of three and five a little girl is given a doll which can be fed by means of a tiny bottle filled with water. The doll will eliminate this water through a tiny hole in its bottom, not quite at the right place, but close enough. Some of these dolls have mechanical devices to reproduce the sounds of a crying baby. Still other dolls can speak sentences from the moment the gift wrapping is removed.

The little girl pretends she is a mommy when she feeds

Betsy Wetsy. The little boy is given toy cars and trucks and he can play "going to work."

It is not good for the little girl or boy in Tribe D to take care of baby brothers and sisters. This is because of "sibling rivalry." It can lead to dropping the baby or abandoning him under a lilac bush.

At puberty, or thereabouts, the girl in Tribe D may graduate to the position of "babysitter." (Since there is no word for "babysitter" in the dialects of Tribes A, B, and C, this is rendered literally and there is an outcry from the delegations of these tribes.) It does not surprise the delegates that a little girl who has learned about babies through playing with a doll should now consider it right to sit on a baby, but what mother in her right mind would permit this? The translation is finally straightened out with dialect renditions which give approximate meaning through the term "baby tender." However, this turns out to be inexact, too. A babysitter in Tribe D is not necessarily a baby tender. Mainly she sits. On a chair. Before the TV.

The baby is usually asleep by the time the sitter arrives. This is prudent since, if the baby were awake, he would tax the arts of the sitter, which have been largely practiced on Betsy Wetsy. On the rare occasions when the baby wakes up, the sitter will have the opportunity to put her early education into practice.

Video: The baby, upon awakening (and expecting his mother), is confronted with a bleary-eyed apparition wearing dental braces. He immediately sets up a howl. This awakens his older sister. She howls, too. The babysitter discovers the baby is wet. No. Worse. She had not counted on this. Betsy-Wetsy wetsies only tap water.

The changing of the diaper occupies 15 minutes. Unlike the docile Betsy, this baby has a built-in bicycle action which thwarts all attempts to position, and to fasten the diaper. He is changed. Is he satisfied? No. The howls reach a higher pitch. He is hungry, the sitter decides. She staggers to the refrigerator and finds a ready-made bottle of formula.

The sitter now feeds the baby. The baby, of course, is made wrong. This is discovered very quickly by the sitter. She positions the baby correctly. If the baby were Betsy Wetsy. The baby is held with his head at a declined angle of 30 degrees, to make sure the contents of the bottle will drain into him. The baby gags, uprights himself, and gives the sitter hell.

The sitter carefully places the baby on the couch and goes away to think. On camera we see the baby thrashing about in a rage. (Watch out, Missy! Don't leave the baby on the couch! He's six months old. He'll go over the edge!)

The sitter is thinking. She has learned to do this in emergencies. (Don't panic. THINK!) She now remembers where she left the phone number. She calls the baby's mother. The baby's mother arrives in time to snatch the baby before he goes over the edge.

How, then, will the girl in Tribe D learn to take care of her own baby when the time comes? It is explained that the girl will be employed many times during the next years as a babysitter and she will practice on other babies. If she does not learn well, or if the babies are the wrong kind of babies, there will be time after her own baby comes to learn everything she will need to know. There are books for the new mother in Tribe D. There is the baby doctor who will answer all the mother's questions, very patiently, very devotedly, on the telephone. There are the mother's own girl friends who have just had babies and have the best up-to-date information on baby care.

"Not the girl's own mother?" asks a Tribe C delegate in astonishment.

"Alas. The girl's own mother in Tribe D is ignorant about today's baby. She has only learned what was right twenty years ago."

"Then does the girl's mother feel ashamed and saddened because she has no wisdom to give her daughter?"

"No. This is because the mother of the mother's mother also had no wisdom to give her daughter in her time. It is a beautiful tradition in Tribe D that the wisdom of one generation should not obstruct the path of the next generation. When a woman becomes a grandmother, she can now fulfill her deepest longings. She can take courses in creative writing and pottery. She can learn to play tennis. She can go to the Land of the Sun every winter."

SESSION #5: BIRTH. CARE OF THE NEWBORN, THE MOTHER, AND THE FATHER

Babies are born at home in Tribes A, B, and C. A woman from the tribe who is very experienced in midwifery attends the mother in labor and during the postpartum period.

The mother of the woman may be present. The husband may be present. In Tribe B specially honored members of the tribe are invited to the birth.

It is a sacred event for the woman and her family. It is believed that if one can say loving words to the mother and embrace her she will not be afraid of the pain and when the baby comes she will have loving words on her tongue for the baby and will embrace him.

When the baby comes, there are cries of exultation from the mother, and from all the attendants at the birth. The baby is placed in his mother's arms at her breast. It is believed that the baby must be received in his mother's arms as soon as possible so that he will know that he is loved. The baby in fact stops his crying and relaxes once he is placed within his mother's arms. The baby's eyes are open. The mother gazes into the baby's eyes and the baby gazes into hers. The mother touches the baby, strokes him with her fingers. She has a lovely smile on her face. The baby snuggles at her breast. His face registers contentment.

This is the way childbirth is described in Tribes A, B, and C. In the immediate postpartum period there are some minor differences in care of the newborn and mother. Thus, in Tribes B and C the baby is put to the mother's breast immediately to encourage sucking and lactation. But Tribe A believes that the first milk is toxic to the baby and "throws it away."

Should the placenta be buried after birth or offered to the Temple? Tribe A cites empirical evidence that a properly buried placenta will insure the survival of the baby and protection of the tribe from floods and disasters. Tribe B has it straight from the deity that She will take offense if the placenta is not presented to the Temple with a traditional sacred prayer.

How shall the tribe protect the newborn infant and the mother against the air which harbors malevolent spirits? Tribe C burns incense to dissipate the lingering spirits and recommends its methods to reduce infant disease and mortality rates. Tribes A and B speak sacred words which they will not divulge at this conference and which drive away the malevolent spirits and reduce the infant mortality rates.

But, alas, the infant disease and mortality rates are very high in Tribes A, B, and C. It is believed that this is because some members of these tribes are careless in the exercise of sacred rituals which, when properly performed, have long protected the tribe against malevolent spirits.

How shall the mother's health be conserved in the postpartum period? Tribe A confines mother and baby to a hammock for forty days. The midwife, the grandmother, relatives, and village matrons attend to the mother, the baby, the husband, and older children. It is also a time to advise the mother on infant rearing, to brew herbal restoratives, and to banish any lingering spirits which have invaded the room of birth. Tribes B and C follow similar practices, but the period of confinement lasts from 14–28 days.

In Tribe D, women deliver their babies in a special place called the delivery room in a hospital. This is because of the danger of microorganisms which can invade the mother and baby. Since Tribes A, B, and C do not have a word for "microorganisms" in their dialects, the polylingual translators substitute the phrase "malevolent spirits." This creates a sympathetic response. The delegates from Tribes A, B, and C are able to follow the doctor's presentation approximately.

Because of malevolent spirits in the delivery room of most Tribe D hospitals, the mother can only be attended by doctors and nurses who wear masks to prevent the spirits from invading the mother and baby. The woman's husband, and her mother, cannot be present because they harbor malevolent spirits.

As this registers with the delegations from Tribes A, B, and C there are outcries.

She is with strangers?

The medical delegate from Tribe D explains that it is better for the woman to be with strangers. The husband and the mother might cause the woman to become nervous and it would not be good for the woman to be nervous. Also, it would cause the doctors and the nurses to become nervous, and that would not be good.

In the delivery room, the woman in Tribe D is placed on her back on a table, with stirrups for her feet. Her hands are tied down and she is wrapped in sheets. There are cries of sympathy from certain delegations. It is explained that this is to prevent the malevolent spirits from entering the woman. The woman does not object because she knows it is right. For her pain and her nervousness the doctors give her soothing medications and vapors.

After the baby is delivered, the nurse shows the baby to the mother. The mother may look at him but she cannot yet hold him. This is because of the spirits in the delivery room. Also the mother has many medicines and vapors in her and

17

she may not remember that she has just given birth to a baby.

The baby is now taken away to a room with glass walls. The mother is taken away to another room on the same floor. This is good because the mother needs to rest and the baby would be bad for her nerves. It is also good for the baby. He will learn to be self-reliant, which is very important for a Tribe D member. He will learn the lessons of solitude, which are highly prized in Tribe D and celebrated in the words of their sages: "When everybody leaves you, brother, you've always got yourself."

In many hospitals in the land of Tribe D it takes twelve hours for the mother to rest her nerves and for the baby to become self-reliant. Then the nurse brings the baby to the mother. The mother rejoices. She is now allowed to hold the baby and to feed him. The father is now permitted to hold the baby. And he rejoices.

The mother and the baby will remain in the hospital for three days. The baby will be brought to the mother every four hours for a feeding. Some mothers will breast feed their babies, and some mothers will feed their babies with the plastic bottle. It is very inconvenient for the nurses when the mother wishes to breast feed her baby. Some mothers decide it is not good to inconvenience the nurses.

The mother has many hours of solitude in the hospital. The baby has many hours of solitude in the room with glass walls. Sometimes the mother cries. This is called the postpartum blues. It is not known why some mothers have the postpartum blues.

A delegate from Tribe B speaks up. In her opinion, she says, the mother is sad in Tribe D because her baby has been taken away from her. The baby does not belong to the mother when he is born. He belongs to the hospital.

There are murmurs of assent from the delegates of Tribes A, B, and C. A mother from Tribe A speaks up. In her opinion, she says, the mother also feels not loved in the hospital. It is not good for a new mother to be among strangers. In Tribe B a new mother has her baby in her arms and the family has loving arms and loving words for the mother to nourish her spirit.

Three days after the Tribe D baby is born, the mother and the baby are allowed to go home. It is a very great moment for the mother and the father. Now they will learn to take care of their baby. Each day the father goes off to work in his car. The mother must now practice feeding the baby, diapering the baby, bathing the baby, and comforting the baby when he cries. She must clean the house and cook the meals and do the laundry.

There are murmurs of protest from the delegates of Tribes A, B, and C. The new mother should rest! Her mother and her aunts and her neighbors should take care of her household.

In Tribe D, it is explained, the new mother does not need to rest. She is very strong. She has had good nourishment throughout her life. She has studied field hockey and tennis in school. She is very self-reliant.

How does the father come to know his baby in Tribe D?

The father in Tribe D has been prepared for fatherhood. When he was a small boy he began to play "going to work" with his little cars. It was not right that a little boy should learn about babies through feeding dolls and, as things turn out, that may be a good thing.

When his wife is in the delivery room, the doctors and nurses give the father a little room to sit in with other men who are about to become fathers. It is necessary to put the fathers away so that they will not make the doctors and the nurses nervous.

The father in his solitude will have much time to think. He is not sure that he has anything to do with the baby that is about to be delivered and must remind himself how babies are made. The father, it is remembered, planted a little seed in the mother. The father's thoughts turn shyly to the act of love which produced this baby and his eyes meet the neutral, competent eyes of nurses who walk briskly down the hall. He feels vaguely ashamed. The fluorescent lights of the waiting room turn the blue plastic furniture into a garish purple. The father puts a coin in the coke machine and wonders what all of this has to do with a night of love.

In the midst of these reveries a nurse appears and calls his name. "A girl! Congratulations!" In the father's mind this is the moment when all the church bells should be ringing and the news should be trumpeted throughout the land. But the stranger who uttered these words seems not surprised; her smile is false and the words are spoken in a flat, cheery voice that is not the voice of angels.

In a little while the nurse appears with a bundle and the father sees a tiny face in the folds of the cloth. He touches the baby shyly. Somehow in the months of waiting he had imagined that in this moment it would be his wife who showed him their baby. They would laugh together and cry together and a circle would close around the three of them. It would be a celebration of love. He feels awkward tenderness for the baby as he peers into her face. He is deeply moved. But he feels—he cannot explain why—he feels as if he were being cheated out of something.

On the morning that he and his wife and their baby are about to leave the hospital he goes to the cashier's office to pay his bill. There is a businesslike exchange over the bill, and the father receives a receipt to be presented to the nursing station which will discharge his baby. He stops at his wife's room. The baby is wrapped in warm blankets. His wife is dressed and ready. The father feels an exultant cry arise in him. He embraces his wife and his baby, and while the roommate looks on—with interest (and the nurse pays no attention)—they dance a little dance together and cry endearments and sing in unison, "She's ours! She's ours!" In this way, the child in Tribe D is twice born.

The delegates from Tribes A, B, C, and D listen to the Tribe D birth story in silence.

A delegate from Tribe D speaks from the floor.

While it is true, says the delegate, that most Tribe D babies are born twice in the manner described, it is important to record in the Congress proceedings that there are experiments under way in Tribe D hospitals in which the baby is born only once.

One experiment is called "rooming in." The mother and the baby go to the same room after delivery and stay together for three days. The baby has a little bassinet next to his mother. The father visits the baby and the mother and can stay for many hours if he likes. However, this experiment is only thirty years old. It is very radical. Only a few hospitals have tried it.

Still another radical experiment is being tried out in certain Tribe D hospitals. The father is permitted to be with his wife during labor and delivery if he wears a mask and behaves himself well. It is, of course, too early to know the results of this experiment.

The delegates from Tribes A, B, and C are astonished to learn that they and their ancestors have been participating in radical experiments, the merits of which have not yet been proved.

At last a young woman rises from her seat in the Tribe D section. She is holding her baby as she stands. She looks competent, sure of herself, and unabashed before this large audience. She looks familiar to the delegates. For a moment, everyone thinks that she is the babysitter of the video story, grown ten years older, with the braces subtracted. But she is not the babysitter, of course. It is only important to realize that she *could* have been the babysitter grown ten years older. She is an experienced mother, all delegates can see.

21

Their practiced eyes observe that she holds her baby with sureness and confidence and that the baby is bright-eyed, alert, inspecting the strangers with caution, and smiling a beautiful smile for his mother.

The young woman speaks in a clear, tempered voice: "There was nothing in my experience as a Tribe D woman that prepared me for motherhood until I became a mother. Yet, I always loved babies and to me and my husband it was a completion of our love for each other.

"I do not think that Tribe D loves its mothers well. A woman like myself who chooses to be a mother is not valued by my tribe. She is often scorned because she has not used her education to improve herself and her tribe. It is thought that anyone can be a mother or a father since this is only an exercise of biological capacity.

"For childbirth, I was exiled in the hospital.

"I do not remember the moment of my child's birth because of the drugs that were given to me. So the celebration which my husband and I had waited for did not come in childbirth, but was postponed.

"I was allowed to see my baby four times a day at feeding time. It was said that I needed to rest my nerves after childbirth. Yet who could judge the state of my nerves better than myself? Hearing a baby cry in the nursery and thinking that it might be my baby was not good for my nerves.

"Finally, after three days my baby and I went home with my husband. After we entered our house, my husband and I embraced each other like two crazy people. We discovered at once that our baby was the most marvelous baby that had ever been born in Tribe D. And he was, you know. Because for some weeks to come my husband and I had to learn how to take care of a baby and he almost never objected to our mistakes."

A speaker from the gallery asks for the floor. He identifies himself as a physician. He would like to begin with a compliment to the previous speaker, he says.

Clearly, he says, his fellow tribeswoman has overstated the case, since she is the mother of a splendid baby who shows no ill signs in spite of his mother's complaints against the hospital delivery and aftercare. And the mother herself, so tender and so competent, may very well serve to justify the very system she deplores.

"She's one of the lucky ones," calls out an anonymous voice from the Tribe D section.

"My dear," says the physician, kindly, to the woman, "medical science has given you a healthy and beautiful child who will live a span of life undreamed of in earlier times. Your great-grandmother had thirteen children and five died at birth or within the first two years. I deplore, as you do, the sterile and cold atmosphere of the modern hospital, but that hospital has given you a live and healthy baby. What else do you want?"

"Everything," says the competent young woman, unabashed. "In my opinion," she says, "a medical science that has brought such progress in the war against the biological enemies of the infant should have the resources—eighty years after the birth of modern psychiatry—to attend to the psychological necessities of a baby and his parents."

This statement brings wild applause from all delegations. The chair declares the meeting adjourned.

A boy's choir, imported by the local chamber of commerce, sings "M is for the million things she gave me." The multilingual translators do not attempt to cope with these verses. Exeunt . . . All.

The Biological Program and Social Tradition

The impossible meeting of delegates from four tribes which we have attended can lead us to these reflections:

Three geographically and socially isolated tribes (A, B, and

C) have more in common with each other in their infant rearing practices than they have with Tribe D, which is technologically the most advanced of these tribes. Also, I have suggested, a great-grandmother in Tribe D would find that her infant rearing methods had more in common with Tribes A, B, and C than with those of her descendants in the late 70's.

These similarities suggest that there are ancient, highly conservative traditions in the human family which have governed the practices of infant rearing and that, for certain reasons, Tribe D departed from these traditions during the 2nd to the 7th decades of this century. The reasons, which we can discern in the Congress proceedings, are themselves related to technological advances which Tribe D has had in its possession. There is every reason to believe that if Tribes A, B, and C had had easy access to the same technology they, too, might have produced changes in their infant rearing practices. However, as representatives of the few isolated and traditional societies which we have available to us for comparison, they can teach us a great deal that has been forgotten.

The subject of this discussion is, after all, the origins of human attachment and of human love, and to pursue the question we are obliged to look dispassionately at the biological and social conditions which facilitate human attachments.

The rigidly conserved patterns of infant rearing we have seen in Tribes A, B, and C are, of course, older than the human race. They are very closely related to infant rearing practices among all primates as we can ascertain through studies of animals in nature.

The baby chimpanzee or monkey, for example, is embraced by his mother soon after birth, and for the entire period of infancy he is cradled in his mother's arms in a close ventral clasp. This is the posture for suckling, for contact comfort, for protection, for grooming, for social exchanges, and for transport. The attachment between the baby chimp and his mother is reciprocal. And it is specific. This body intimacy leads the infant to discriminate his mother and to seek proximity to the mother even when his own mobility begins to give him some degree of independence. The mother's attachment to her baby is also specific. The baby is an active partner in attachment; he elicits nurturing and protective behaviors in his mother.[4]

Accidental (or experimental) separations of the baby and his mother lead to panic states in both mother and child. Infant monkeys, during prolonged separations from their mothers, suffer grief and mourning states that cannot be distinguished from those seen in human infants. Pathological behaviors will occur as the infant settles into a stuporous state.[5]

Also, as we all know now, an infant monkey experimentally deprived of a mother of his species, reared as in Harlow's experiment on dummy mothers, will become an aberrant animal. Among the causes isolated in Harlow's experiments are the deprivation of tactile-kinesthetic experience normally given in the ventral cradling by the mother and the psychological deprivation of a mother who is a partner, actively responding to signals from her baby, providing comfort and—to use the awkward phrase of our science—providing stimuli for the activation of sensorimotor systems in the infant.[6]

In short, the biological program which insured the survival of the young also insured mutual attachment between mother and infant. In the evolutionary course of our own species, the matrix of these affectional systems remained the same, with the important difference that the father in the human family became an important figure in his own right in the development of human bonds.

In the social traditions of infant rearing which are conserved in Tribes A, B, and C we can see the biological pattern as structure beneath the social patterns. The biological synchrony of suckling, tactile intimacy, cradling, comforting, sensory arousal, and communication through signs are rigidly conserved through custom in these traditional societies.

It was not necessary for a mother in Tribes A, B, and C to know that each of the components of this intricate pattern was designed to insure the primary human attachments in infancy. If the mother followed tradition (and if tradition was rigidly transmitted from one generation to another), she produced under all normal circumstances a child who showed all the favorable signs of human attachment at two years of age.

If we search for a single word that underscores this discourse on attachment and love, the word "intimacy" is most apposite. We cannot imagine a human attachment in which intimacy between the partners is not a condition. The traditional patterns of birth and nurture of the infant have the virtue of providing the optimal conditions for intimacy. (A woman in labor attended by loved persons; a baby placed in her arms; a baby at the breast; a prolonged period of lying in, in which the baby is at his mother's side; the breast feeding which unites the baby and his mother for his nourishment and their mutual satisfaction; the prolonged period of breast feeding, and the transporting of the baby in a close ventral position.)

Now of course, if a social experiment in infant rearing modifies any component of this intricately complex biological system, it will have effects upon contiguous and interlocking systems. If, for example, we isolate a mother and her baby in the post-partum period, which normally provides the optimal conditions for closeness, intimacy, and fulfillment, we are taxing the parents and their baby to find that completion through their own resources after the homecoming. It is a testimonial to parental love that most parents and most babies in Tribe D will "make it," but for many parents those first days or weeks are strained because the consummatory moment of parenthood was postponed in the hospital.[7]

If the bottle is substituted for the breast, the biological necessity for the infant to experience intimacy in a close ventral clasp must be compensated for through the mother's intelligent knowing or her intuitive understanding that the baby needs both food and love in her arms. It is no longer "built in" to the program. The majority of mothers in Tribe D who employ bottle feeding approximate the breast feeding position in their bottle feeding of the baby. But there are many mothers today who feed their babies by means of a propped bottle in his crib, or who present the bottle to the baby while he reclines in a plastic seat. There are many solitary babies today who do not know the sensual delights and comfort of the embrace. Since it has been amply demonstrated that body intimacy in the embrace is essential for the psychological and physiological organization of the infant, the baby of an unknowing mother can be deprived of essential nutriments for his constitution and for the conditions of attachment.

Whereas the breast necessarily, automatically, binds the baby to a specific person, his mother, the bottle does not guarantee this union. The mother who "knows" or "intuits" her baby's need for her as a central person will prefer to take over most or all of the feedings herself. The mother who does not "know" is easily led into the circumstance where "anyone" can give the baby his bottle. There are some babies in Tribe D who are fed by "anyone handy" in a large household or an indifferent day-care center, and these babies do not seem to discriminate their mothers from other persons at an age where most babies show preference for and valuation of the mother.

The bottle gives a mother far more mobility than the breast, which is one of the reasons for its growing popularity during the past fifty years. The breast was "intended" to bind the baby and his mother for the first year or two years of life. If we read the biological program correctly, the period of breast feeding insured continuity of mothering as part of the program for the formation of human bonds. A baby today experiences many more separations from his mother than the baby in traditional breast-feeding societies. How does this affect the stability of the bonds to mother?

In short, where the biological program evolved to insure intimacy and attachment between the baby and his mother and where the conservative social traditions maintained the program, the practices in infant rearing in Tribe D offer options which may or may not provide the essential nutriments for human attachments. It is now the wisdom of the mother which insures the integrity of human bonds. And since many parents in Tribe D are bereft of the traditional baby wisdom which was once transmitted through grandparents, they are adrift in a sea of conflicting advice from experts, from neighbors, and even from a vocal faction of women in the tribe who decry the "slavery" of motherhood.

Human Attachment: Putting the Story Together

If the reader finds himself at this point with the sensations of jet lag in this story that leaps from biology to social traditions in infant rearing, from folklore to science and science to folklore, it may be the fault of my exposition, but it is also a fair equivalent of the experience of science itself in unraveling the story of human attachments.

This chapter began with an imaginary dialogue between me and my grandmother in which we touched upon some of the scientific findings which bear upon the development of human bonds in infancy. My grandmother seemed not surprised by a summary of major findings. Most mothers and fathers would consider them unspectacular. When we discuss the "language of love" in infant development nearly every parent can recognize the signs. Yet the scientific work goes far beyond the discovery of what is obvious. The importance of this work lies in "putting the story together," in finding meaning, coherence, and design in the sequence of events.

If we now come back to the "language of love" which we have identified through signs in infancy, we will find extraordinary parallels between the "dialogue" of love between an infant and his first partners and the universal vocabulary of love which we normally celebrate as an experience *de novo* in adult life.

During the first six months, the baby has the rudiments of a love language available to him. There is the language of the embrace, the language of the eyes, the language of the smile, vocal communications of pleasure and distress. It is the essential vocabulary of love before we can speak of love. Eighteen years later, when this baby is full grown and "falls in love" for the first time, he will woo his partner through the language of the eyes, the language of the smile, through the utterance of endearments, and the joy of the embrace. In his declarations of love he will use such phrases as "When I first looked into your eyes," "When you smiled at me," "When I held you in my arms." And naturally, in his exalted state, he will believe that he invented this love song.

The baby's rudimentary love language belongs to an innate repertoire. It is all there, potentially, in the program, but it must be elicited by a partner. (In the rare and tragic cases in which a baby is deprived of mothering he will not gaze into the eyes of a partner, he will not smile, or rarely smile, he will not vocalize, and he will resist the arms of anyone who attempts to hold him.)

The baby who is reared in normal circumstances begins to show preference and valuation for his mother and his father around six months of age, or earlier. We can discern this through the same sign language. He seeks the eyes of his mother, he smiles more frequently for his mother than for strangers, he vocalizes more frequently for his mother than for strangers, he prefers to be held by his mother and will resist the arms of strangers. (All love, even in later life, begins with a feeling of exclusiveness. "You are the one who matters; only you.")

And now between six months and fifteen months the baby begins to show his love in new ways. He complains when he is separated from his mother for a few hours. He's very likely now to pucker up when he sees his mother in her hat and coat, and sitters may report that he cries for a time after she leaves. The baby has discovered that his mother is, for the time being, the most important person in his world. And he behaves the way all of us behave when a loved person is leaving for a journey, or is absent for a while. ("I can't bear to be without you. I am lost. . . . I am not myself without you. . . . You are my world and without you the world is empty.")

If all this seems too extravagant to put into the minds of babies, we need only watch a baby of this age whose mother has been called away on an emergency for several days, or a baby who has been isolated from his mother in a hospital. The face of grief is no different at eight months of age from what it is at thirty years. Loss of appetite, sleeplessness, refusal of comfort from someone else—all this is the same.

From this short sketch we can see that already at the end of the first year, the baby has gone through a sequence of phases in his human attachments: from simple recognition of the mother, to recognition of her as a special person, to the discovery that she is the source of joy, the satisfier of body hungers, the comforter, the protector, the indispensable person of his world. In short, he has learned to love.

N.B.

For those rare babies who have been deprived of mothers or mother substitutes—babies in institutions, for example—there is no sorrow at the disappearance of a human figure or the absence of another person. Since no one person is valued above others, all people are interchangeable.

Between one and two-and-a-half years of age, the baby who has formed a deep attachment to his mother is also moving toward some degree of independence and autonomy. His own mobility brings him to explorations of the world around him. He tends to go off on brief excursions around the house or the yard, then return to "touch base" with his mother. She is the safe and comforting center and must continue to be so for some years to come. And now, too, he is an active partner in affectionate exchanges. He will initiate the hugs and kisses with his parents as often as they do.

He can tolerate brief separations at two-and-a-half more easily than he could at one year. But prolonged separations for several days will still create anxiety in him. The anxiety is a measure of his love and a measure of his incapacity, still at two-and-a-half, to grasp fully the notion that a mother, though not present, must be someplace and will certainly return. He can hold on to this notion for a few hours, or a day or two, and then, if his mother does not magically reappear and confirm her substantial existence, he reverts to a more archaic notion: she is lost, he is lost. And he behaves exactly as older people do when the lover has deserted. He cries, he buries his head in the age-old posture of grief, he casts off the advances of well-meaning friends, he cannot rest, and he has no appetite.

From all this we can see that a human infant has within him all the human capabilities for profound and enduring attachments and the full gamut of emotions which we read as signs of love and loss.

The pathways that lead from infant love to the love of maturity can be outlined in this story.

Love of a partner and sensual pleasure experienced with

that partner begin in infancy and progress to a culminating experience, "falling in love," the finding of the permanent partner, the achievement of sexual fulfillment.

In every act of love in mature life there is a prologue which originated in the first year of life. There are two people who arouse in each other sensual joy, feelings of longing, and the conviction that they are absolutely indispensable to each other—that life without the other is meaningless. Separation from the other is intolerable. In the wooing phase and in the prelude to the act of love, the mouth is rediscovered as an organ of pleasure and the entire skin surface is suffused with sensual joy. Longing seeks its oldest posture, the embrace.

In the first falling in love, every pair of lovers has the conviction, "Nothing like this has ever happened to me before; I never knew what love could be." And this is true, but only in a certain sense. The discovery of the partner, the one person in the world who is the source of joy and bliss, has its origin in the discovery of the first human partner in infancy. What is new is the *new* partner and the experience of genital arousal with longing for sexual union. Yet the pathway to full genital arousal in mature life was laid down in infancy, long before the genitals could play a dominant role in experience. It was the infant's joy in his own body, the fullness of infant sensuality, that opened the pathways to genital fulfillment in maturity.

Freud said all this seventy years ago, and there were few who believed him.

CHAPTER II

The Origins of Human Bonds

THE BONDS that unite human partners are older than man. We neither invented the bond nor own the exclusive rights to it. The enduring ties that join members of a species in couples, in groups, and in complex social organizations exist in many species other than our own.

Stable and permanent partnerships for the propagation of young can be found among some species of fish, and these partnerships endure beyond the period of spawning and raising of the young. Among greylag geese there are elderly couples which have raised their broods and remain demonstrative to each other and solicitous of each other's welfare in an exclusive and cozy domesticity that outlives the biological purpose of the union. Lorenz has described genuine grief reactions among widowed geese. Similar accounts exist of the fidelity of jackdaw couples, even after prolonged separation.

In this chapter I propose to pursue the biological story with particular reference to the work of Konrad Lorenz, and to examine the relationship of love and aggression which Lorenz puts before us in his book, *On Aggression*.[1] The biological story illuminates many problems in human psychology and brings us back to the central issues of human attachment which were posed in Chapter I.

On Aggression and the Bond

Within the same species that produce permanent bonds among members, *fighting* among members is also a common occurrence. The fighting is regulated by formal rules of conduct and ritual forms of triumph and appeasement. It seems that the "problem" of aggression, which we like to believe was invented by the moral intelligence of man, is no less a "problem" to every species that possesses the bond!

Conflicts between the claims of love and the claims of aggression did not originate with our own intelligent species. The devotion and fidelity of the greylag goose, for instance, is maintained through elaborate rituals which are designed to divert aggression from the partner. Even the device of the scapegoat appears in a simplified form among some species of fish, and is ubiquitous among species that exhibit bond behavior. To put it simply, aggression is channeled *away* from the partner in order to preserve the bond.

The parallels between these phenomena and the data of human development and human behavior are striking. In the course of his development, the child modifies his aggressive urges through love of his human partners. In the case of a child who has been deprived of human partners in the formative years he may lack inhibitions of aggressive impulses or extraordinary problems in the regulation of his aggression.

In the psychoanalytic view, conflicts between love and hate are central in the human personality. The modification of aggression in the service of love has produced an infinite variety of redirected actions and mental mechanisms which serve to discharge drive tendencies through substitute goals. It has produced in man great love, great work, and the highest moral attainments. And while the same conflicts between love and hate can also produce neurotic symptoms in the human personality, it is well to remember that modification of aggression—through sublimation, for example—can bring successful solutions to these conflicts without resorting to disease.

Naturally, at a time when the most intelligent of animals seems bent on the extermination of his own species, a study of the natural history of aggression and its relationship to the love bonds would prove instructive. This is not to say that the solutions that have evolved among sea animals and birds are applicable to human society. When Lorenz urges us to regard the lessons from biology with modesty, he is not suggesting that we employ the rituals of waterfowl to regulate our daily aggressions or our foreign policy. He is telling us that there is an evolutionary tendency at work which has produced ever more complex and effective means of regulating aggression, that this tendency is at work within human society in ways that we cannot easily recognize without following the biological narrative, and that at this point in our history there are as many portents for solutions to the ancient problems of human aggression as there are portents of disaster.

The Paradox

At the center of Lorenz's book is a paradox. (1) Intraspecific aggression—fighting among the members of the same species—is a characteristic of some species but not of others. (2) *Yet the bond appears only in those species which also manifest intraspecific aggression!* (3) There are species that have intraspecific aggression and no bond, but conversely, there are no species that have the bond and do not also have intraspecific aggression. (4) Within those species which have evolved enduring attachments among members, there are biological mechanisms for inhibiting aggression under certain conditions and there are ritual forms of courtship and greeting ceremonials among members in which the characteristic motor patterns of aggression have undergone a transformation in the service of love.

It appears, then, that there are phylogenetic links between aggression and love. The coexistence of intraspecific aggression and the bond in certain species should inform us of the biological purpose and earliest interdependence of two instinctual drives which have evolved as polar and antagonistic. This is the territory that Lorenz explores.

Among the human psychologies, psychoanalysis maintains its position with regard to the instinctual drives. In 1920, when the earlier libido theory was modified by Freud, aggression was given full status as an instinctual drive; a two-drive theory (sexual and aggressive) has remained central to psychoanalytic theory since that time. While recent advances in psychoanalytic theory have been in the area of ego psychology, psychoanalytic ego psychology has, on the whole, remained firmly rooted in biological foundations. It is the ego's role as a regulator of drives, the ego as the agency of adaptation, the ego as the mediator between drives and the demands of conscience, that define ego for psychoanalysis.

Now, it matters a great deal whether we include drives in our theory or not. If we believe that an aggressive drive is part of the biological inheritance of man, we add another dimension of meaning to conflict. It means that we grant motivational force to aggression that can, at times, be independent of objective circumstances. We thus are able to explain what the behaviorists cannot well explain, the ubiquitous conflicts of love and hate, the admixture of aggression in the most sublime love, the "store" of aggression in human personality which can be triggered by a militant slogan or a boxing match or the buzzing of a mosquito. In this view the aggressive drive is given; it cannot be abolished—although it can be brought into the service of human aspirations by inhibiting those of its tendencies of the drive that can lead to destructive purpose.

We can learn, then, from the study of biology that the biological "purpose" of aggression is not murder. The killing of a member of one's own species is rarely encountered outside of human society. When it occurs among animals in the wild state, it is accidental. When it occurs in a zoo or an animal laboratory it can be demonstrated that some component in the instinctual organization was deprived of a nutriment which is vital for functioning or of the stimulus for release, and that the intricate network which transmits signals within the instinct groups broke down. In one example given by Lorenz, hens that were surgically deafened for experimental purposes killed their newly hatched chicks by furious pecking. The hen, who does not "know" her young, normally responds to the call notes of the newly hatched chicks, which elicit appropriate maternal behavior. The deafened hens, unable to receive the signals of their young, reacted to the stimulus of the "strange object" and unleashed aggression—heightened in this period by the necessities of brood defense—against the brood itself.

Lorenz defines aggression as "the fighting instinct in beast and man which is directed *against* members of the same species." Intraspecific aggression usually occurs in the service of survival. By warding off competitors within the species, aggression maintains living space and an equitable access to the food supply. Aggression is essential for defense of the brood; in any given species the primary tender of the brood, whether male or female, is endowed with the highest amount of aggressivity. With some rare exceptions, intraspecific fighting is limited to subduing the opponent or causing him to take flight. Lorenz describes ritual expressions of appeasement and submission in the loser of the fight as well as ritual forms of triumph (the "triumph ceremony") in the winner. Lorenz and other ethologists have collected thousands of examples from various species and have analyzed the components of each action in order to determine the specific patterns and variations. Each species, it appears, has its own forms of appeasement and triumph, and the ritual performance becomes a common language in which each gesture, each subtle nuance, has a sign function that is "understood" by every other member of the species. Among wolves and dogs, for example, the submissive gesture is the offering of the vulnerable, arched side of the neck to the aggressor. This is by no means an analogue to a "death wish" in the animal; it is the signal, "I give up," and it derives its function as a signal from the opposite behavior in fighting in which the animal protects the vulnerable region by averting his head. The triumph ritual among dogs is the lateral shaking of the head, the "shaking-to-death" gesture with mouth closed. At the end of this ceremony, the loser retreats and the victor marches off.

This ritualization of innate aggressive patterns is one of the most important links between instinct and the social forms that derive from instinct. The motor patterns for aggression are innate; when another instinct is manifested simultaneously, or when external circumstances alter its aim, the innate motor pattern is still produced but with some slight variation that endows it with another function and another meaning that is "understood" in the common language of the species.

What prevents a fight to the death within a given species? By what means can an animal check the intensity of his aggression before he destroys a member of his own species?

There are inhibitions in animals, Lorenz tells us, that are themselves instinctive in their nature. There are inhibitions against killing an animal of one's own species or eating the flesh of a dead animal of the species. Nearly all species have inhibitions against attacking females or the young of the species. These inhibitions are so reliable that Lorenz regards a dog who attacks a female as aberrant and warns the reader against trusting such an animal with children. As we follow Lorenz we see that certain values which for humans are "moral imperatives" have antecedents in the instinctual inhibitions of animals.

Now if we grant that a certain quantity of energy is expended in an aggressive act, an inhibition of aggressive action can leave a quantity of undischarged energy in an animal that does not have a repertoire of behaviors or mental mechanisms for blocking discharge. In this dilemma the most common solution among animals is "redirection," to use the ethological term. That is, the animal switches his goal and discharges aggression on a substitute object. In one of many examples given by Lorenz, a female fish wearing the glorious colors of her "nuptial dress" entices a male. In the cichlid, the colors worn by the female are also the very colors that elicit aggression in the species. The excited male plows toward the female, clearly intent on ramming her. Within a few inches of the female he brakes, swerves, and directs his attack to a hapless bystander, a male member of the species. The foe vanquished, the victorious fish presents himself to his bride in a triumph ceremony, which serves as a prologue to the sexual act.

In this example, the inhibition is provided by the claims of another instinct, the sexual drive, and discharge of aggression is redirected toward another member of the species—an "indifferent object," as we would see it. This is a very simple example of conflict between two drives in a species less complex than our own. The claims of each drive must be satisfied, but the aggressive drive cannot satisfy itself upon the sexual object without obstructing the aim of the sexual drive. Redirection of the aggressive drive toward substitute goals provides the solution.

We can, of course, immediately recognize the behavior of "redirection" as a component of human behavior: in its simplest form it is analogous to "taking it out" on another person or an indifferent object, "displacing" the anger. Among humans the behavior of "redirection" has evolved into complex mental mechanisms in which drives are directed to substitute aims, as in sublimation, in defense mechanisms, and also at times in symptoms. In striking analogy with the drive conflicts of the unintelligent animals, it is the necessity among humans to divert aggression away from the object of love that creates one of the strong motives for the displacement, inhibition, and even repression of aggressive impulses. This means, of course, that the mental mechanisms available to humans not only permit redirection of the drives toward objectives that are far removed from "motor discharge of aggression," but that energy is available for investing the substitute act with meaning far removed from "the fighting instinct." Where aggressive and sexual impulses enter into a work of art, for example, the original impulses undergo a qualitative change and the product in the work itself becomes a metaphor, a symbolic representation of the biological aims.

I do not wish to strain the analogies between "redirection" in animals and in humans. When complex mental acts intervene between a drive and its expression, as in human behavior, we are clearly dealing with another order of phenomenon. It is, for example, the human capacity for symbolic thought that makes it possible for the ego to block discharge of a drive or, more marvelous still, to exclude from consciousness (as in repression) the idea associated with the impulse. In non-human species, where there are no ideas and, properly speaking, no state that corresponds to "conscious-ness" in humans, there are no equivalents for repression.

Yet, we will find it arresting to see, in Lorenz's animal data, simple forms of symbolic action, a preliminary sketch for a design that becomes marvelously extended and elabo-rated in human thought. This is the process called "ritualiza-tion" in animals which we have already touched on in con-nection with the ceremonies of appeasement and triumph in animals. Lorenz presents us with an impressive body of data to show how courtship ceremonies among many species have evolved through the ritualization of aggression.

Any one of the processes that lead to redirection may be-come ritualized in the course of evolution. In the cichlid we saw earlier how aggression against the female is diverted and discharged against another member of the species in the courtship pattern. Among cranes there is a kind of tribal greeting and appeasement ceremony in which "redirected aggression" is simply pantomimed. The bird performs a *fake* attack on any substitute object, preferably a nearby crane who is not a friend, or even on a harmless goose, or on a piece of wood or stone which he seizes with his beak and throws three or four times into the air. In other words, the ritual redirection of aggression has evolved into a symbolic action.

Among greylag geese and other species, the redirected fighting and its climax are ritually observed in courtship, but they have also been generalized into a greeting ceremonial within the species as a whole. Greylag geese, male or female, greet each other ritually by performing the triumph cere-mony. It is the binding ceremony of the group, and the per-formance of this rite with another member of the group renews and cements the bond, like the handshake or pass-word of a secret society or a tribal ceremonial.

And here we reach the central part of Lorenz's thesis, the evolution of the personal bond. We recall that Lorenz and other ethologists have demonstrated that personal ties among members of a species—"the bond"—appears only among species in which aggression against members of the same species also occurs. Using the greylag goose as a model, Lorenz shows how redirected forms of aggression become ritualized, then follow an evolutionary course to become the binding force among members of the group. Thus, among the greylag geese, a species with strong intraspecific aggression, there are stable and enduring friendships and lifelong fidelity between mates. These are bonds which are relatively independent of survival needs or procreation. Unlike partnerships found in some other species, these bonds are not seasonal or circumstantially determined. The mate, the friend, among greylags is individually recognized and valued; he cannot be exchanged with any other partner. Loss of the friend or mate produces genuine mourning in the bereaved partner. And the ceremonial that binds these birds in pairs and in groups, the ritual greeting, the ritual wooing, the bond of love, is the triumph ceremony which originated in fighting and through redirection and ritualization evolved into a love ceremonial which has the effect of binding partners and groups. Aggression is made over in the service of love.

In the model of the greylag goose, Lorenz traces the pattern of the triumph ceremony in fine detail. The phylogenetic origins of the pattern are probably similar to those described in the cichlid: that is, a conflict between the subject's sexual aims and aggressive aims toward the same object finds a solution in the redirection of aggression toward another, an "indifferent" object. The pattern evolved as a condition for mating and, through ritualization, became part of the courtship ceremonial. In the further evolution of the ritual fight, the triumph ceremony acquired a sign function for the affirmation of love; within the species it became a binding ritual. The ceremony, as Lorenz points out, has become independent of sexual drives and has become a bond which embraces the whole family and whole groups of individuals, in any season.

Lorenz adduces a large number of examples to show the evolution of greeting rituals from the motor patterns of aggression. Among certain birds, the "friendly" confrontation and exchange of signals is barely distinguishable from the threatening stance and gestures of the same species (thus, for example, the expressive movement which accompanies cackling among geese). But close observation and motivational analysis show a detail, such as a half-turn of the head or body, which alters the "meaning" of the motor pattern so that the sign value of the pattern is taken as friendly. The human smile, Lorenz suggests, probably originated in the same way: the baring of the teeth in the primal threatening gesture has been made over into the friendly smile, the uniquely human tribal greeting. No other animal has evolved the act of smiling from the threatening gesture of tooth baring.

Moreover, these greeting patterns, which are found among all species that have personal bonds, are not dependent upon learning. Given certain eliciting stimuli, the baby animal produces the greeting sign as part of his innate inventory of behaviors. If one bends over a newly hatched gosling, says Lorenz, and speaks to it "in an approximate goosy voice," the new-born baby goose utters the greeting sound of its species! Similarly, given certain "eliciting stimuli," the human baby in the first weeks of life produces our tribal greeting sign, the smile.

All of this means that in the process of redirection and the ritualization of aggression in the service of love, a new pattern emerges which acquires full status as an instinct and a high degree of autonomy from the aggressive and sexual instincts from which it derived. Not only are the patterns of love part of an autonomous instinct group, but they have a motive force equal to or greater than that of aggression under a wide range of conditions, and are capable of opposing and checking and redirecting aggression when the aims of aggression conflict with those of love.

While we can speak, then, of innate tendencies that produce characteristic forms of attachment in a particular species, it is very important to stress that these patterns of attachment will not emerge if certain eliciting stimuli are not provided by the environment. In the case of the newborn gosling, the cry of greeting is elicited by the call notes of the species, usually provided by the mother. Lorenz, by producing these sounds experimentally, elicited the greeting sounds from the newborn gosling and actually produced in hand-reared geese a permanent attachment to himself; he became the "mother." In experiments which Lorenz describes in *On Aggression* and elsewhere, he was able to produce nearly all of the characteristics of early attachment behavior in young geese by providing the necessary signals during the critical phase of attachment.

In other experiments in which baby geese were reared in isolation from their species and otherwise deprived of the conditions for attachment, an aberrant bird was produced, a solitary creature that seemed unaware of its surroundings, unresponsive to stimuli—a creature, in fact, which avoided stimuli as if they were painful. It is worth mentioning in this context that Harry Harlow in certain experiments with monkeys accidentally produced an aberrant group of animals with some of the same characteristics of stimulus avoidance.[2] In his now famous experiments in which baby monkeys were reared with dummy mothers (a cloth "mother," a wire "mother") the animals became attached to the dummy mothers in a striking parody of the species' attachment behavior, but the animals also produced a group of pathological symptoms that were never seen among mother-reared monkeys. They were strangely self-absorbed, made no social contact with other members of the species, would sit in their cages and stare fixedly into space, circle their cages in a repetitive, stereotyped manner, and clasp their heads in their hands or arms and rock for long periods. Some of them chewed and tore at their own flesh until it bled. When these animals reached sexual maturity they were unable to copulate. In the rare circumstance under which a female could be impregnated by a normal male from another colony, the female ignored her young after birth or tried to kill them.

To those of us who are working in the area of human infancy and early development, these studies of attachment behavior in animals and the correlative studies of animals deprived of attachment have had a sobering effect. For there are some striking parallels between them and our own studies of normal development and of certain aberrant patterns in early childhood which I will describe later as "the diseases of non-attachment." In all these studies of animal behavior and human infancy, we feel as if we are about to solve an ancient riddle posed by the polar drives of love and aggression.

The Diseases of Non-Attachment

In the earliest years of psychoanalysis, Freud discovered that conflicts between the claims of love and the claims of aggression were central to all personality development. As early as 1905 he demonstrated through the study of a five-year-old boy, "Little Hans," how the animal phobias of early childhood represent a displacement of aggressive and libidinous impulses from the love objects, the parents, to a symbol of dangerous impulses, the animal.[3] The phobia served the function of keeping the dangerous impulses in a state of repression and of preserving the tender feelings toward the

45

parents in a state of relative harmony. This is not to say, of course, that conflicts between drives must lead to neurotic solutions. There are other solutions available in childhood, among them the redirection of hostile impulses in play and in the imagination. But in all these instances of normal development and even in the case of childhood neuroses, the motive for the redirection of hostile impulses is love. *It is because the loved person is valued above all other things that the child gradually modifies his aggressive impulses and finds alternative modes of expression that are sanctioned by love.*

In all this we can see an extraordinary correspondence between the regulation of human drives and the phylogenetic origins of the love bond as constructed from the data of comparative ethology. Perhaps it might even strike us as banal to say that human aggression should be modified by love. We are accustomed to take human bonds as a biological datum in human infancy. There would be no point in writing this chapter if it were not for another story that is emerging from the study of a large body of data in psychoanalysis, psychiatry, and psychology on the diseases of non-attachment.

The group of disorders that I am here calling "the diseases of non-attachment" are, strictly speaking, diseases of the ego, structural weaknesses or malformations which occur during the formative period of ego development, the first eighteen months of life. These disorders are not classified as neuroses. A neurosis, properly speaking, can only exist where there is ego organization, where there is an agency that is capable of self-observation, self-criticism, and the regulation of internal needs and of the conditions for their expression. In a neurosis there may be disorders in love relationships, but there is no primary incapacity for human attachments. Similarly, we need to discriminate between the diseases of non-attachment and psychoses. In a psychosis there may be a breakdown or rupture of human bonds and disorders of thinking which are related to the loss of boundaries between "self" and "not self"—all of which may testify to structural weaknesses in ego organization—but this breakdown does not imply a primary incapacity for human attachments.

The distinguishing characteristic of the diseases of non-attachment is the incapacity of the person to form human bonds. In personal encounter with such an individual there is an almost perceptible feeling of intervening space, of remoteness, of "no connection." The life histories of people with such a disease reveal no single significant human relationship. The narrative of their lives reads like a vagrant journey with chance encounters and transient partnerships. Since no partner is valued, any one partner can be exchanged for any other; in the absence of love, there is no pain in loss. Indeed, the other striking characteristic of such people is their impoverished emotional range. There is no joy, no grief, no guilt, and no remorse. In the absence of human ties, a conscience cannot be formed; even the qualities of self-observation and self-criticism fail to develop. Many of these people strike us as singularly humorless, which may appear to be a trifling addition to this long catalogue of human deficits, but I think it is significant. For smiling and laughter, as Lorenz tells us, are among the tribal signs that unite the members of the human fraternity, and somewhere in the lonely past of these hollow men and women, the sign was not passed on.

Some of these men and women are to be found in institutions for the mentally ill, a good many of them are part of the floating populations of prisons. A very large number of them have settled inconspicuously in the disordered landscape of a slum, or a carnie show, or underworld enterprises where the absence of human connections can afford vocation and specialization. For the women among them, prostitution affords professional scope for the condition of emotional deadness. Many of them marry and produce children, or produce children and do not marry. And because tenderness or even obligatory parental postures were never a part of their experience, they are indifferent to their young, or sometimes "inhumanly cruel," as we say, except that cruelty to the young appears to be a rare occurrence outside of the human race.

A good many of these hollow men remain anonymous in our society. But there are conditions under which they rise from anonymity and confront us with dead, unsmiling faces. The disease of emotional poverty creates its own appetite for powerful sensation. The deadness within becomes the source of an intolerable tension—quite simply, I think, the ultimate terror of not-being, the dissolution of self. The deadness within demands at times powerful psychic jolts in order to affirm existence. Some get their jolts from drugs. Others are driven to perform brutal acts. We can learn from Jean Genet of the sense of exalted existential awareness that climaxes such acts. Victims of such acts of brutality are chosen indiscriminately and anonymously. There is no motive, as such, because the man who has no human connections does not have specific objects for his hatred. When caught for his crimes, he often brings new horror to the case in his confession. There is no remorse, often no self-defense. The dead voice recounts the crime in precise detail. There was no grievance against the victim: ". . . he was a very nice gentleman. . . . I thought so right up to the minute I slit his throat," said one of the killers in Truman Capote's *In Cold Blood*.[4]

Among those who are driven to brutal acts we can sometimes see how aggression and sexuality are fused in a terrible consummatory experience. It is as if the drives themselves are all that can be summoned from the void, and the violent discharge of these urges becomes an affirmation of being, like a scream from the tomb. Yet it would be a mistake to think that such criminals are endowed with stronger sexual urges than others. For the sober clinical truth is that these are men without potency and women without sexual desire, under any of the conditions that normally favor sexual response. These men and women who have never experienced human bonds have a diffuse and impoverished sexuality. When it takes the form of a violent sexual act it is not the sexual component that gives terrible urgency to the act, but the force of aggression; the two drives are fused in the act. When we consider the ways in which, in early childhood, the love bond normally serves the redirection of aggression from the love object, we obtain a clue: the absence of human bonds can promote a morbid alliance between sexual and aggressive drives and a mode of discharge in which a destructive form of aggression becomes the condition under which the sexual drive becomes manifest.

From these descriptions we can see that the diseases of non-attachment give rise to a broad range of disordered personalities. But if I have emphasized the potential for crime and violence in this group, I do not wish to distort the picture. A large number of these men and women distinguish themselves in no other way than their attitude of indifference to life and an absence of human connections.

The hollow man can inform us considerably about the problem we are pursuing, the relations between the formation of human love bonds and the regulation of the aggressive drive. In those instances where we have been able to obtain histories of such patients, it appears that there were never any significant human ties, as far back as memory or earlier records could inform us. Often the early childhood histories told a dreary story of lost and broken connections. A child would be farmed out to relatives, or foster parents, or institutions: the blurred outlines of one family faded into those of another, as the child, already anonymous, shifted beds and families in monotonous succession. The change of address would be factually noted in an agency record. Or it might be a child who had been reared in his own family, a

family of "no connections," unwanted, neglected, and sometimes brutally treated. In either case, by the time these children entered school, the teachers, attendance officers, or
school social workers would be reporting for the record such
problems as "impulsive, uncontrolled behavior," "easily
frustrated," "can't get close to him," "doesn't seem to care
about anything." Today we see many of these children in
Head Start programs. These are the three- and four-year-olds
who seem unaware of other people or things, silent, unsmiling, poor ghosts of children who wander through a
brightly painted nursery as if it were a cemetery. Count it a
victory if, after six months of work with such a child, you can
get him to smile in greeting or learn your name.

Once extensive study was begun on the problems of unattached children, some of the missing links in etiology appeared. We now know that if we fail in our work with these
children, if we cannot bring them into a human relationship,
their future is predictable. They become, of course, the per-
manently unattached men and women of the next generation. But beyond this we have made an extraordinary and
sobering discovery. An unattached child, even at the age of
three or four, cannot easily attach himself even when he is
provided with the most favorable conditions for the formation of a human bond. The most expert clinical workers and
foster parents can testify that to win such a child, to make
him care, to become important to him, to be needed by him,
and finally to be loved by him, is the work of months and
years. Yet all of this, including the achievement of a binding
love for a partner, normally takes place, without psychiatric
consultation, in ordinary homes and with ordinary babies,
during the first year of life.

This brings us to another part of the story, and to further
links with the biological studies of Lorenz. Research into the
problems of attachment and non-attachment has begun to
move further and further back into early childhood, and fi-

nally to the period of infancy. Here too it is pathology that has led the way and informed us more fully of the normal course of attachment behavior in children.

Clinical Studies: Lost and Broken Attachments in Infancy

Since World War II, a very large number of studies have appeared which deal with the absence or rupture of human ties in infancy. There is strong evidence to indicate that either of these two conditions can produce certain disturbances in the later functioning of the child and can impair to varying degrees the capacity of the child to bind himself to human partners later in childhood. A number of these studies were carried out in infant institutions. Others followed children who had spent their infancy and early years in a succession of foster homes. In each of the studies that I shall refer to here, the constitutional adequacy of the baby at birth was established by objective tests. When control groups were employed, as they were in some of the studies, there was careful matching of the original family background. These investigations have been conducted by some of the most distinguished men and women working in child psychoanalysis, child psychiatry, and pediatrics—among them Anna Freud, Dorothy Burlingham, René Spitz, John Bowlby, William Goldfarb, Sally Provence, and Rose Lipton.

The institutional studies have enabled us to follow the development of babies who were reared without any possibility of establishing a human partnership. Typically, even in the best institutions, a baby is cared for by a corps of nurses and aides, and three such corps, working in shifts, have responsibility for large groups of babies in a ward.[5] The foster-home studies, on the other hand, together with studies of "separation effects," have enabled us to investigate a group of babies and young children who had known mothering and human partnerships at one or another period of early development and who suffered loss of the mother and often repeated separations from a succession of substitute mothers. In one set of studies, then, the groups of babies had in common the experience of no human partnerships; in the other, the babies had suffered ruptures of human ties in early development.

Within these two large groups the data from all studies confirm each other in these essential facts: children who have been deprived of mothering, and who have formed no personal human bonds during the first two years of life, show permanent impairment of the capacity to make human attachments in later childhood, even when substitute families are provided for them. The degree of impairment is roughly equivalent to the degree of deprivation. Thus, if one constructs a rating scale, with the institution studied by Spitz[6] at the lowest end of the scale and the institution studied by Provence and Lipton[7] at the other end of the scale, measurable differences can be discerned between the two groups of babies in their respective capacities to respond to human stimulation. But even in the "better" institution of the Provence and Lipton study, there is gross retardation in all areas of development when compared with a control group, and permanent effects in the kind and quality of human attachments demonstrated by these children in foster homes in later childhood. In the Spitz studies, the degree of deprivation in a hygienic and totally impersonal environment was so extreme that the babies deteriorated to the mental level of imbeciles at the end of the second year and showed no response to the appearance of a human figure. The motion picture made of these mute, solemn children, lying stuporous in their cribs, is one of the little-known horror films of our time.